THREE PATHS,
THREE CHOICES

THREE PATHS, THREE CHOICES

GETTING THE LIFE THAT YOU DESERVE

SHERRY D. RANSOM

iUniverse, Inc.
New York Lincoln Shanghai

THREE PATHS, THREE CHOICES
Getting The Life That You Deserve

iUniverse books may be ordered through booksellers or by contacting:

iUniverse
2021 Pine Lake Road, Suite 100
Lincoln, NE 68512
www.iuniverse.com
1-800-Authors (1-800-288-4677)

ISBN-13: 978-0-595-38537-9 (pbk)
ISBN-13: 978-0-595-82915-6 (ebk)
ISBN-10: 0-595-38537-0 (pbk)
ISBN-10: 0-595-82915-5 (ebk)

Printed in the United States of America

To my husband, Alfred, a constant source of encouragement and love. To all of my readers, a prayer for new enlightenment and new dreams.

It's a Matter of Choice

The matter of grace,
The matter of choice,
We get them so confused.

The only thing they have in common

Is that neither can be overused.

Grace opens the door and makes a way,
While choice comes along to define the day.

Refusing to choose is laughing at grace,
And telling God, 'No, thank you,' right to his face.

Whether you live or whether you die, it's a mat-
ter of grace.
How you live before you die, it's a matter of choice.

Choose well.

Sherry D. Ransom

The Discovery Paths

Acknowledgments

Special thanks to my proofreaders, Alfred Ransom, Laura Osborn Saldivar, and Lee Moczygemba. Your thoughts and comments guided my hand and helped bring this dream to fruition.

I extend my gratitude to Ellen Smith, who always kept me on the upward path. Your ability to see the gift of manifestation in my life is a gift that I treasure.

I am also thankful to my children, Duane and Tanya Johnson, who have always supported my many, many dreams.

To my mother, Verna Chatman, all of my love. I finally understand your journey.

The Journey Begins

For almost forty years, the process of succeeding and living my dream life has been a persistent challenge. I became intrigued by the difference between living a good life versus living a great life more than thirty-seven years ago when I met a girl who would become my personal challenger. When I first saw her in Dallas, Texas, I had no idea that she would become such a huge inspiration in my life. I was a senior in high school, headed for college in the fall. My life changed the moment I saw her because she had something that I had never seen before. She was vibrant, self-assured, pretty, and so full of life that she seemed to be in perpetual motion, while I stood transfixed, wrapped in a cloak of shyness and dastardly self-awareness.

The year was 1966, and our paths crossed because our respective high schools were scheduled to clash in a final game for the state football championship. I was a member of a crowd of onlookers during a pep rally, and she was one of the cheerleaders for her Houston, Texas, high school team. Our eyes met—I would always remember her, and she instantly forgot me. I told myself that I could never have that sparkle of life and self-assuredness that she possessed, although I wanted it so badly. After the pep rally, I felt quite sure that we would never meet again, but destiny had other plans.

That fall, I left home for the first time and traveled to Washington DC to enroll in college. There were only two Texans assigned to my dorm floor in Crandall Hall—me and the former Houston cheerleader. I learned that her name was Debbie Allen. Although we lived on the same floor, we never formally met. We passed each other in the hall and attended the same freshman welcoming activities. Our eyes met again during a freshman boat ride on the Potomac. My eyes captured every detail, including exactly what she was wearing, and her eyes glanced past me as if I were not really there. I arrived at college with no goal in mind other than to leave my unloving home. She arrived at college with the goal of becoming a theatrical wonder.

I was not alone in my fascination with her. Soon, the other girls on the floor began to talk about her loving and supportive family and about a picture album that she had that showcased her early achievements in life. It was even rumored that her mother had been an accomplished poet and that Martin Luther King had actually visited her home. I was not surprised to find that she fascinated the other girls as well. When I heard of her loving and supportive family, I had my excuse. I could never succeed the way she would because I lacked the love and support of my family. The wheels for my mediocre journey were solidly affixed to my wagon of life.

I did not know then what I know now. You become the person you believe you will be. I never tried to choose a career or major in college. Instead, I settled for a major in English literature based on nothing more than I loved to read the literature of the period. Sadly, during that time, I needed to prove that I was lovable more than I needed life goals. Consequently, I sought a husband while she sought a career.

After college, I followed her career in magazines and news reports. Every time I reached a milestone in my life, she mirrored a different one. I would go along for a few years and forget about her, then I would begin to tackle one of life's obstacles and she would be there on my television or in a magazine, smiling and successful. There were times when she seemed to be everywhere I looked. She starred in and directed movies, opened the Academy Awards more than once with stunning choreography, and starred in a television program aptly named *Fame*. While she was being honored with both Tony and Emmy awards, I continued to use the crutch of lack of family love and support as an explanation for never leaving the starting gate.

During the next thirty or so years that passed, I became a closet writer and observer of others who had followed their dreams to success. I penned two novels, many short stories, and even poems. They never saw the light of day. In time, I had grandchildren and wrote a children's story for their entertainment, which they loved so much that each summer when they visited, they asked for the next installment. I began to think of publishing, but held back, and then it happened. My personal challenger wrote and published a children's book. Why her and not me?

The possibility of succeeding had a firm grip, and I began to interview successful people and quietly take notes about the behaviors of those who succeed. The same message came through repeatedly: first believe, and then act as though you believe.

I finally had it. The difference between me and my personal challenger had always been that <u>she believed in her ability to achieve her dreams</u> and <u>I didn't believe in myself</u>. I decided that was going to change. So, I tested my theory.

First, I decided to go after a dream I had treasured for more than twenty years by opening my own gift shop. I set a plan in motion, believed in my success, and within a year opened one of the most beautiful stores I had ever entered. For a full year before the store opened, I believed and acted as though I believed. I took classes, wrote a business plan, and scouted locations and vendors. I still needed to pass another test.

Like many women all over the world, I was a daily viewer of the *The Oprah Winfrey Show*. In autumn 2000, I submitted a letter asking to appear on the show to discuss a book club selection. I mailed the letter and believed as strongly as I could. It happened! I was selected to be a guest. After that television appearance, I met so many people who wanted to know how to make a dream come true that I decided to research and write a book that laid a solid plan for success—this book.

However, I had more to learn. My gift shop closed after being open for a year because I still lacked the knowledge needed to sustain and nurture my dream. I went into a period of despair until my personal challenger again crossed my path. She was invited to come to town as a shining example of a successful Texan in the world of entertainment. My period of despair transformed into a period of self-discovery. This time, I knew that success could also be mine. I now knew that I had to take many steps to reverse the patterns I had set by not believing in myself. These steps are carefully laid out in this book. What I discovered is that success is not a one-time decision. It is a daily commitment. You, too, can succeed by choosing your possibilities on a daily basis. Living your dream life is a journey of self-discovery that you will treasure. Thank you for choosing this book, and thank you, Debbie Allen, for never letting me forget that success is a matter of choice.

What can I do in the next 15 minutes to help my dream come true?

I am a money making machine

Part I
Choosing

Welcoming the Power of Choice

"Every human has four endowments—self-awareness, conscience, independent will, and creative imagination. These give us the ultimate human freedom.... The power to choose, to respond, to change."

Stephen R. Covey
Author of *The 7 Habits of Highly Effective People*

The Three Paths

Checkered, Yellow, or Green — You Choose

"Understand that the right to choose your own path is a sacred privilege. Use it. (Dwell in possibility.)"

Oprah Winfrey, *O, THE OPRAH MAGAZINE*

What choice do you have? All of the choices in the world!

For far too many years, I lived my life under two false beliefs. The first belief was that my environment limited my choices. The second belief was that I could change my circumstances by making a one-time decision to plunge forward. I was wrong on both counts. I eventually learned, as you will, that my choices are limited by my beliefs and actions and that my progress toward living my dreams is a daily choice rather than a declaration of purpose.

We have all listened to the promises of motivational speakers who advocate that if you decide to change, it can be accomplished. You leave their lectures pumped with enthusiasm but ill equipped to go beyond that first declaration of change. Their declarations are true, but with one very large caveat—change is a daily decision, and you need supportive tools to succeed. I have found that creative change is a daily decision that becomes a string of decisions that form years, decades, and, ultimately, your life.

> Every moment in life reflects either a choice that has already been made or an opportunity to make a new choice.

Each morning, whether you like it or not, you are faced with choices that ultimately determine the outcome of your day. You make choices from the moment you open your eyes, even if you believe that you can't possibly think before your first cup of coffee. Many people believe that they are not making *any* choices; they merely go through the motions of living. However, by the time you have that first cup of coffee, you may have made as many as twenty choices that will impact your day and your life.

Throughout the day, you will continue to make choices, both consciously and unconsciously. Sadly, many people believe that life offers no choice or that their choices are limited. Every moment in life reflects either a choice that has already been made or an opportunity to make a new choice. Luckily, as an adult, you are the one who gets to choose.

Confusion reigns when you consider *unconscious choice* as not being a choice at all. Choices made unconsciously have just as much impact as choices you have weighed and made consciously. For this book, we'll discuss the following two choices: conscious choice and unconscious choice.

Conscious choice—You make decisions after weighing the outcome and consequences. Any possible impact on your happiness and success in life are included in the decision-making process.

Unconscious choice—You make decisions in reaction to previous choices without weighing any new elements that may affect the outcome and consequences. Happiness and success in life are left to chance and to the choices made by others.

Although I often use career choices as examples in this book, your life choices are not limited to career choices. Life choices are actually happiness choices. As an example, if you choose to become a hermit in the woods and it brings you happiness, do it! Backpacking across Europe is a happiness choice that has no career connections. You can choose to write poetry for your own enjoyment, or you can choose to be the best mother or father possible. The point is that you need to make a conscious choice to find your own state of happiness.

You alone are responsible for finding your key to happiness and enjoyment. No other person can choose your state of bliss. If you are unsure of the path you want to take, use the exercises in this book to help you find your path.

First, you must acknowledge the blessing of choice as being tantamount to success in life, since you will make choices consciously or unconsciously. The goal is to make conscious choice your impetus. As soon as you awaken each day, you can choose from three distinctly different paths that can set not only the pattern for your day, but also your feelings of happiness and success. The three paths of opportunity that await you each day are the Checkered Path, the Yellow Path, and the Green Path:

The Checkered Path: *You choose not to choose.* It is a choice that seems relatively low risk, but it is fraught with surprises. Why? You have given control to the forces of the universe. Your five senses are dulled, and your sixth sense is tuned to a low frequency. The only goal you have is to survive another day.

There is no consistency, and those on this path tend to feel as if they are being moved along life's journey like game pieces, subject to the whims of the other game players.

People who choose the Checkered Path consistently feel like they are on a treadmill. They fear change because it represents a frightening unknown. They can look back over their lives and see very little change over the decades and very little happiness.

The Yellow Path: *You choose to continue living the low-risk yesterday.* Whether you lived yesterday in a state of happiness or depression, you believe that, by reliving it again today, there will be no surprises. Any fulfillment you experience is fleeting because there is no real pattern or goal for the choices you make. Your sixth sense is tuned to a higher frequency, but you often choose to ignore feelings that can be categorized as gut feelings or intuition. You're stuck in a rut of your own making.

Yellow is the color of caution, patience, and lack of courage. This path is yellow because the people who choose this path fear change, momentum, and decisions. They make choices consciously, but weigh the consequences in a state of fear.

People who choose the Yellow Path can look back over their lives and see moments of happiness. Only after careful review do they realize that those moments of happiness occurred when they made conscious choices to be happy, such as taking vacations, going to concerts, or making unusual purchases.

Remember, life is too short to live the same day twice!

The Green Path: *You choose to live a life of purpose.* You make choices with your eyes on a specific goal. You weigh your choices for their effect on tomorrow's goals. It may seem extremely risky, but it is not. You are making choices based on your vision, and you have weighed the risks. Happiness is part of the goal and is attainable. Your sixth sense is highly tuned, and you pay attention to random events. Choices made on this path lead to mounting satisfaction.

We call people who choose the Green Path achievers. They know where they are going, and they have some idea of how to get there. These are the people who circumvent the situations into which they were born. <u>Their happiness in life out-weighs their unhappiness.</u>

When counseling others, I cannot state this enough: you are not your career! It is unfortunate that Americans tend to define themselves by their career choices. While it is true that, in certain situations, a career choice can dictate happiness, there are other situations in which career choice breeds discontent. I have chosen to be a writer and inspirational speaker after many other career choices. I find happiness in writing and speaking. That happiness makes me a better wife, mother, and friend. On the other hand, there are people who write for a living who dread every assigned interview. They remain on the same old treadmill for many reasons, including a desire for a pension, a lack of incentive to change careers, or a fear of starting over. Their unhappiness at work impacts their other roles in life.

Let's take a look at the lives of three people and the choices they are making:

Sabrina

Sabrina is a twenty-five-year-old woman who lives in Seattle, Washington. She is unhappy in her job as a paralegal in a large law firm. Her <u>dream i</u>s to be a singer, and she feels stuck in her present situation. Her life is not unhappy. She has friends, a boyfriend, and a comfortable condominium in a well-established part of the city, but she feels like something is missing.

What is missing in Sabrina's life is her dream. She sees herself as a woman with limited rather than unlimited choices. Sabrina no longer chooses to choose. She lets life happen.

It is 6:00 AM, and the alarm clock in Sabrina's bedroom is sounding the beginning of a new day.

She will make many choices before leaving for work. You cannot live your life without making choices. Choosing not to get out of bed is a choice. Sabrina's choices include the following:

- ❑ Turning off the alarm
- ❑ Getting out of bed
- ❑ Showering
- ❑ Washing her hair
- ❑ Wearing makeup
- ❑ Brushing her teeth
- ❑ Deciding what to wear
- ❑ Making the bed
- ❑ Eating breakfast
- ❑ Drinking coffee
- ❑ Going to work

The choices listed above could quadruple before she arrives at work, since every moment of our lives involves making choices. Those choices determine our attitude for the day, our appearance, our health, and our overall well-being. After leaving home and having made more than one hundred decisions, Sabrina begins another workday. She will not make any choices during the day that will lay a path to her dream life of being a singer. Perhaps a miracle will occur during the day that will catapult her into her dream life, perhaps not. Sabrina has unconsciously chosen the Checkered Path.

Mitchell

Mitchell lives in Atlanta, Georgia. He is a tax attorney who went to law school to appease his father, who is also an attorney. He earns a comfortable income and lives in an upscale neighborhood. He could change his life if he wanted to. Mitchell has always loved cooking, and his best moments are after work when he prepares gourmet meals and dazzles his large group of friends. Occasionally, he entertains the idea of enrolling in a culinary school and pursuing his passion for cooking, but his father would never understand.

Mitchell's daily choices are carefully made to include no change from the day before. He has chosen to live a good life versus his best life. His life is carefully planned to avoid change.

- ❑   Morning shower, coffee, dress
- ❑   Drive to work—same route
- ❑   Planned workday
- ❑   Dinner with friends on Friday (every Friday)
- ❑   Dinner with parents (every Saturday night)
- ❑   Yard work—Saturday mornings
- ❑   Church (Sunday)

Every day Mitchell chooses to relive yesterday. He consciously chooses not to pursue his dream. It seems to be a low-risk choice. If Mitchell continues to repeat yesterday and lives a long life, he will probably regret choosing not to step outside the box and take a chance on his dream. Mitchell has consciously chosen the Yellow Path.

Elizabeth

Elizabeth is a photographer who lives in Chicago, Illinois. After college, she accepted a position with a large firm as a structural engineer. During high school, she had two passions—mathematics and photography. She chose the career that promised a solid financial future. After five years of working as an engineer, she decided she wanted to try photography again after viewing some vacation photos she had taken. It began as a hobby and blossomed into a career more lucrative than engineering. Best of all, Elizabeth feels happy and fulfilled with her new career choice.

Changing careers did not happen quickly; it took four years for Elizabeth to achieve her dream of being a professional photographer. Elizabeth had to make choices that supported her decision to change careers. She had to do the following:

- ❑ Buy camera equipment
- ❑ Take photography classes at local colleges
- ❑ Set up a darkroom at home
- ❑ Buy darkroom equipment
- ❑ Decide who and what the subjects of her photos would be

- ❑   Save money for downtime during her career change
- ❑   Join a local photography club
- ❑   Arrange to travel with the club for group photo shoots

Elizabeth's first book of photos has just been published and is being praised by critics. Elizabeth chooses the Green Path every day.

Which person do you most clearly identify with?

I lived my life cautiously, choosing to walk the first two paths for decades. I believed that if I was a good person, life would reward me—I only had to wait for the opportunity to show itself. Once I chose the Green Path, two things happened to change my mind: I opened a retail store, and I made a guest appearance on *The Oprah Winfrey Show*. At that point, my life took on new meaning, and the universe opened doors for me.

No one lives on the Green Path every day. You will spend random days on the Yellow or Checkered Paths. This becomes a problem only when you remain on either the Yellow or Checkered Path long enough to establish a pattern of thinking that no longer supports your dreams. I have spent most of my life on the Yellow Path, fearing change and fearing success. Choosing the Green Path daily required a change in my thinking patterns.

You too can choose the Green Path. You need a certain tool set to help you reverse your old thinking patterns. Your inability to make good, conscious choices is often blocked by those negative affirmations I call the Pretenders. Choosing the

Green Path on a daily basis requires confronting and conquering self-defeating feelings that are blocking your progress. In the chapters that follow, you will meet and learn how to defeat the Pretenders.

love it!

"It is a funny thing about life. If you refuse to accept anything but the best, you very often get it."

William Somerset Maugham
English playwright, novelist, and short story
writer (1874–1965)

The Pretenders

Mine Fields on the Paths

"If you can find a path with no obstacles, it probably doesn't lead anywhere."

Frank A. Clark

One of the reasons you have not chosen the Green Path in the past is due in part to the presence of feelings I call the Pretenders, since they <u>pretend to have your best interests at heart,</u> but they are actually <u>limiting factors</u> in your life.

Imagine for a moment that you decide to become a writer. You've chosen this dream because you enjoy writing and it gives you more comfort than any other activity. You finally make a conscious choice to become a professional journalist.

At the precise moment you make the decision to pursue a career as a writer, the Pretenders go to work. They whisper words of discouragement, such as:

- ☑   You don't have enough education.
- ☐   You won't be any good.
- ☑   You aren't as good as you think.
- ☐   You have plenty of time. Wait a few years.
- ☐   Stick to what you're trained to do.
- ☐   You need connections to get a publisher. Don't be foolish.

The Pretender voices will continue until you either take control or weaken and change your direction back to the status quo. The Pretenders challenge your desire to pursue your dream. On most days, if you have chosen the Yellow Path, you will give up and continue on yesterday's path. You will have lost the challenge. If you're unaware that the Pretenders are working against you, you might assume that they are looking out for your best interests by keeping you from being disappointed when you fail.

I have lived with and listened to the Pretenders for more than fifty years. I have allowed them to discourage me from trying to reach my dream time and time again. I escaped their taunts by shining a light directly on them. These pages are proof that I am living a major part of my dream. I'm a writer and professional speaker and, from this point forward, nothing will stand in my way.

You too can live your dream. Neither age nor economic factors can hold you back. You've already begun by taking this journey with me through these pages. Together, we will chase the Pretenders out of your life by shining a light so brightly on them that they dare not appear.

Disguises of the Pretenders

The most disconcerting thing about the Pretenders is that they look just like you, and their voices sound just like yours. This makes it very difficult to see them as enemies. They are parts of you—parts that have grown larger over the years as you listened to their voices and reacted by shelving your true desires. You're fooled because you want to believe that the Pretenders have your best interests at heart. The Pretenders are *not* your friends. See if you recognize any of your Pretenders in the following disguises: fear, perfectionism, procrastination, shyness, and regret.

Pretender #1—Fear

Fear will convince you that:

❑ There is not enough money available to support your dream.
❑ You are not worthy of your dream.
❑ You do not have time for your dream.
❑ Your dream is silly and not worth pursuing.

I once knew a gifted musician named David who could play any wind instrument, but his true talent blossomed when he played the tenor saxophone. David grew up in the small town of Waco, Texas. He was well known for his captivating solos. I often wondered why he played in small venues when he had such a big talent. I asked, and he reluctantly told me a story about a missed opportunity. One night, during a concert in Waco, he was so drawn into the jazz number being presented that he began to solo on each of the band instruments, even the keyboard. The other band members simply stood back and listened in awe.

Opportunity knocked that night when David was offered the chance to tour with one of the best horn sections in the music business. The band's manager, who had witnessed David's performance, was anxious to add such a powerful talent to his group. David's dream of traveling all over the world to showcase his talent had materialized. He remembers becoming violently ill right after meeting the band manager. He took it as a sign that he should pass on the opportunity.

Although David dreamed of traveling and playing before huge audiences, he declined. Fear convinced him that he wasn't good enough and needed more training.

The decision he made that evening haunted him for years. It killed something inside of him. He knew in his heart that he should have trusted his talent and training. Sadly, he could not overcome his fear of the unknown. David lives his life on the Yellow Path.

The last time I saw him, he was still mastering his talent and drawing crowds to watch him play two tenor saxophones at once. He still played in small venues and had tucked his dream into his back pocket, resigned to never live his dream of traveling and playing before large crowds.

Fear is the most recognizable Pretender in your life. When fear arrives to counsel you, it often is accompanied by a strong, adverse physical reaction. This physical reaction is often so strong that you will avoid taking any steps that might summon a repeat performance. Your heart may race, you may experience shortness of breath, and you may even become physically ill.

Fear can take many forms, including guilt, self-loathing, denial, and depression. The one trait they all have in common is that they become limiting factors in your life. Fear often partners with the other Pretenders—perfectionism, procrastination, shyness, and regret; however, they all have their own peculiarities.

I have been writing for more than ten years. Until recently, I called myself a closet writer. I finished two novels and several short stories and magazine articles. For a great deal of that time, fear kept me from sending manuscripts to publishers. I would rewrite a novel over and over again, using different narrators and different voices. Fear always whispered, "It's not good enough." "You need more education." "It's not literary enough." "Why are you setting yourself up to fail?" "Why can't you be happy with your life as it is?"

I would stop writing for months at a time and try to convince myself that the desire to write was just a pipedream, but it would always return with an even greater urgency. I would read a bestseller and realize that I had better plots tucked away in a drawer. After a few months, I would drag myself back to the computer and begin again. Fear would wait until I decided to come out of my closet, then it would walk in and sit beside me to begin its litany of reasons not to try.

You may have a different dream, yet fears of failure and ridicule have held your dream at bay, just as they held mine. This book explores various ways to banish the shadows of fear from your life, so that you can continue the journey toward making your dream a reality.

Pretender #2—Perfectionism

Perfectionism will convince you that:

- ☑ The timing is not perfect.
- ☐ The necessary money is not available.
- ☐ It's not worth angering family or friends.
- ☑ You need to build your dream model over and over again, forever seeking perfection.

Have you ever had a great idea, and while you slowly developed and tested it in your mind, someone else presented it to the world? This has happened many times to me. There are those who believe the universe will present you with an idea, but, if you delay developing it, the idea will be presented to someone who will take action on it.

Many would-be writers set out to write the next Great American Novel. They often succeed, but their desire for perfection delays the project for years, sending it through numerous rewrites, character changes, and plot turns. During each change, a little of the writer's self-confidence dissolves until there is none left in the project, and it becomes a large stack of papers tucked away under the bed or in a desk drawer. Quite often, not another living soul has had the opportunity to read the manuscript and comment on its worthiness. The need to write a perfect novel that needs no editing becomes a dream killer.

The world almost missed the opportunity to enjoy one of the greatest books written by Dr. Norman Vincent Peale. When he was in his fifties, Peale finished a manuscript into which he had poured his heart and soul, but he was unable to find a publisher. With the encouragement of his wife, Ruth, he had rewritten the book several times. In frustration, he tossed the manuscript into a trashcan and told his wife not to remove it. The next day, Ruth picked up the trashcan and delivered it and the manuscript to a publisher. After the publisher finished laughing at the unusual form of delivery, he read the manuscript. He was impressed by the general theme of the book and suggested that it be renamed *The Power of Positive Thinking*. The book was published and became one of the premier bestsellers in history with more than 20 million copies printed in forty-two languages.

Many inventions are also lost to the public while the inventor seeks perfection before submitting the idea for patent. The inventor becomes so intent on achieving perfection that he loses sight of the fact that he can patent the idea and make changes or additions later.

Nothing else you have accomplished in your life is 100 percent perfect, but you may convince yourself that every aspect of your dream must be. This allows you no room for mistakes or second thoughts because the planning of your dream must hit no snags. You think that you *must* have plenty of money to begin accessing your dream, and your family and friends *must* be 100 percent supportive for you to continue. As you research the steps necessary to fulfill your dream, if you encounter *any* obstacles, you put your dream on hold, often permanently.

Perfectionism is a Pretender that will delay your dream and push your goal further and further out of reach. I challenge you to recognize the goal of perfectionism as a Pretender, especially if it has hindered your progress in pursuing your dream. <u>Recognition is the key to fighting this Pretender.</u>

Recognizing and acknowledging that your quest for perfection is delaying the delivery of your idea can be very liberating. Once I acknowledged that no manuscript had ever been delivered in a form that required no editing, I took the enormous amount of time I had been spending in rewrites and channeled that energy into delivering this book to the public. It was not easy or instant, but my persistence and ability to refocus helped me break the habit of seeking perfection.

The road to living your best life won't be entirely smooth. There will be detours and potholes along the way that often provide worthy lessons. There may be times when you don't have the complete picture in your mind and your realized dream will only slightly resemble your original vision. Detours can steer you in directions that help you in unimaginable ways. Don't look for perfection. Be open to change. After all, no script ever makes it to the screen without editing!

Other people in your life may limit you by making you think perfectionism is important. These people are stumbling blocks to your dreams. Recognize their desires as detours rather than aids, and foil their negative impact on your life. Neither you nor your actions have to be perfect to proceed.

Fight perfectionism by: ?ro -vision

- Sharing your dream with supporters.
- Recognizing low self-esteem as the motive for delay.
- Accepting change as a part of life.
- Not confusing detours with stop signs.
- Being determined to share your dream with the world!

The Pretender perfectionism has a close companion that often takes on the guise of perfectionism to delay a vision from maturing. It's called procrastination.

Pretender #3—Procrastination

Procrastination will convince you that:
- There is always another time.
- You are too old to start anew.
- You need to complete more steps to proceed.
- Your time would be better spent on another project.

I have a talented friend named Sylvia, who makes fabulous jewelry using native stones and gold wire. Her booth at church bazaars and local festivals is always the most popular one. She has researched the nature of the stones and can tell you which stones will bring you luck, courage, or love. Sylvia often talks about showing her jewelry to a wider audience. Unlike many people who abandon their dream, Sylvia has taken advanced classes in jewelry making and marketing.

She has everything she needs to succeed, except the ability to beat her Pretender—procrastination. A buyer for a prestigious nationwide hotel gift shop saw Sylvia's jewelry at a bazaar and offered to showcase it in the hotel's shops nationwide. Sylvia panicked and asked if she could call the buyer back in a few days. She used those few days to convince herself that she needed to take more classes and to amass more stones—that she simply could not make time for such a venture.

This is a talent that Sylvia has carefully cultivated for more than fifteen years. Her big break arrived, and she called the buyer to decline. Fear and the need to procrastinate caused her not only to miss out on the opportunity, she also put away her jewelry making tools for more than two years.

The effects of procrastination plague everyone from time to time. Fear leads to procrastination and, inevitably, to regret, creating a vicious cycle that can kill any dream.

Procrastination is a difficult habit to break. Yes, it *is* a habit, and it's important that you recognize it as such. When opportunity knocks, *now* is the time to act—not later! Recognizing the voice of procrastination is the first step. I broke my habit of profound procrastination by removing the word *later* from my vocabulary when it pertains to an action I must take. "Later" has no real time identification. If I postpone an action, I give it a definite time for completion and follow through. Twenty-one days of action will break any habit.

To break the habit of procrastination;
- ❑   Make a commitment to act now.
- ❑   Assign dates to your activities.
- ❑   Remove the words 'later' and 'tomorrow' from your vocabulary.
- ❑   Make daily lists and cross items off as they are completed.
- ❑   Make no promises that you can't keep.
- ■   Seize opportunities as they present themselves. Waiting will only cause the opportunity to disappear.
- ❑   Avoid people who aid you in procrastinating by taking you off course.
- ■   Reward yourself for completing an activity or list.

The voices of the Pretenders will grow weaker as you follow these steps to banish procrastination from your life. With procrastination behind you, you are free to plan your dream life.

Pretender #4—Shyness *Bill Goss*

Shyness will convince you that:

- ☐ Nice people don't demand respect.
- ☐ You shouldn't get involved in confrontations.
- ☐ Just trying is good enough.
- ☐ Life and its gifts will come looking for you.
- ☐ You should accept the status quo although you have more to offer.

Years ago, there was a popular piano player who drew a steady crowd to the hotel bar in his city. He performed elegantly, whether he accompanied a singer or played solo tunes. His tip bowl, which sat prominently on his piano, was always full by the end of each evening. He could play any tune requested, regardless of its musical genre. Being a shy man, he felt both secure and anonymous behind the piano. When he played the piano, he didn't need to interact with the bar's patrons other than to smile and nod as they made song requests or placed tips in the bowl. The piano player always shunned the spotlight, even in later years when he became a celebrity.

One evening, the bar manager insisted that the piano player sing as he played. When the piano player declined, the manager insisted that he sing or find another job. With a family to support and no confidence that he would find another job, he acquiesced and sang. He eventually became famous for his voice, with his piano playing being only a backdrop.

He sold more than fifty million records during his lifetime. The name of that piano player is Nat King Cole.

For many years, I missed opportunity after opportunity to advance in life due to shyness. I even ascribed a cloak of honor to my shyness by labeling myself as meek and gentle. My cloak of shyness let me play the victim with a smile.

Shy people are not winners or achievers if their shyness overshadows their innate abilities. Shy people are unable to look another person in the eye, speak up for themselves, articulate their needs, or live life to its fullest. No one is born shy. It is a state of being that people adopt to avoid confronting fearful situations. Shy people see confrontation of any sort as a negative encounter. With each avoided confrontation, they grow shier, and eventually their shyness begins to justify its existence. Life should not be embroiled in constant confrontation, but confrontations can test your mettle and define your strengths.

Walking through life wearing a cloak of shyness has its consequences. Your shyness can become so strong that you can't leave its embrace to pursue the things you truly desire. You may have donned the cloak of shyness to avoid confrontation with a parent, but it is not easily thrown off when you want to catch a suitor's eye or need to be more aggressive to get a deserved promotion!

 Methods for overcoming shyness include:

- ❑ Taking risks—start with small activities that make you uncomfortable and build up to larger activities.
- ❑ Practice making eye contact with others. It will be difficult at first but it does get easier.

- ❑ When conversing with others, shift your thinking to their comfort rather than yours.
- ❑ Congratulate yourself for each effort to come out of your shell—even if you did not get the response you expected.
- ❑ Give yourself one daily task to accomplish that is out of character.
- ▣ Try making eye contact and speaking a warm salutation to coworkers each day. This really works and I practice it each day on total strangers.
- ▣ Before any gathering, spend extra time in the mirror to ensure that your appearance is acceptable, so that you can shift your thoughts to others.
- ❑ Reward yourself for even the smallest accomplishments.

Shyness is not a virtue. It is a choice, a choice that limits what you do with your life. Choose to be proactive about pursuing the things in life that you truly want.

Pretender #5—Regret ℬ𝒢

Regret will convince you that:
- ❑ It's too late to follow your dream.
- ❑ Only peak physical conditioning is acceptable to follow your dream.
- ❑ Yesterday is more important than today.
- ❑ Having enough money is the most important element of your dream.

Regret is the most adamant Pretender in the mind of those who are older. However, this Pretender is not limited to them. It can also strike fear in the young, causing golden opportunities to be lost.

It is *never* too late to follow your dream. The list of those who achieved their dreams late in life is almost endless. Some examples include Dr. Albert Schweitzer, Grandma Moses, Kenny Rogers, Booker T. Washington, Dr. Norman Vincent Peale, Eleanor Roosevelt, Morgan Freeman, and Albert Einstein.

Dreams can be modified to fit current physical conditions. If you're older or physically unable to achieve your dream in its original form, you can set new standards, so you can continue to follow your dream. The Senior Circuit did not always exist in the world of professional golf. It was established by golfers who did not want to stop living their dream due to age restrictions.

If your dream is to be a lawyer, law schools accept students at any age. Modify your dream to incorporate your knowledge and volunteerism if the qualifications for the activity are highly physical. Better yet, start a "senior" branch of the activity. I would enjoy watching a group of grandpa clowns at the circus. They might not be as physically fit as the younger clowns, but they would probably be a lot more innovative in their antics. My point is, only you can choose to stop pursuing your dream!

Time is an elusive character. Yesterday is not more important than today. In fact, yesterday is less important, because you can no longer make any changes to it. Today is a fresh canvas waiting for you to apply the brushstrokes that will ultimately color your life. Choose your colors carefully, apply the brushstrokes gently and with love, and frame the canvas with your passion, and yesterday will be what it really is—a memory.

Comparing yesterday to today has no validity. Everything has changed. Your body, mind, experiences, and wisdom regarding the world are all different. Whenever yesterday starts to affect today's decisions, remember the old phrase, "That was then, and this is now."

I am often asked during speeches about the process of wading through the hurts and heartaches of yesterday. The hurts remain because they have not been addressed. In most cases, they have been shoved into a dark corner and acknowledged only to carry the negative feelings we harbor from one time period into another. When you are faced with heartache, feel it, then analyze not only its impact on your life, but the situations that might have led to its occurrence. Were there different choices you could have made? Was there a lesson for you to learn? Did its original negative impact become a positive force in your life? Would you do the same thing all over again?

Great Questions

There are certainly tragedies over which we humans have no control. These include the death of loved ones, disease, car accidents, plane crashes, and so on. These are not regrets that you simply get over. Major regrets that we can overcome are loss of jobs, divorce, broken relationships, anger over harsh words and deeds, and anger over imagined slights. These regrets have no place in our lives, unless we choose make a place for them to reside.

amazing!

> *"Let your hopes, not your hurts, shape your future."*
>
> Dr. Robert H. Schuller

Another question I am often asked is, "How do we honor the past and not remember the hurts?" The answer is: acknowledge the hurts and refuse to give them permanent reign over your present and future choices. Regret has no positive connotation, except when it leads to gratitude for the lesson!

There are two forms of regret. In one form, an experience is used as a litmus test for the rest of life's experiences in a negative way. I have a friend whose mother felt that life dealt her a bad hand. Her mother used that regret to teach her children that life is a fearful condition and that challenges are punishments and 'bad luck.' She raised a family that fears every decision and one that takes no risks in life. Their lives are a mirror of hers. The difference is that the children's lives were manufactured not by the Creator or their own life experiences, but by the negative outlook of their mother. Maternal encouragement is something that my friend has never experienced. She is working hard to break the negative cycle and teach her own children to see their life experiences as lessons rather than punishments. Her mother still sees her own life as a hardship, although she is relatively comfortable and constantly surrounded by friends and family.

The other form that regret can take is as an impetus to improve or capitalize on one's life experiences. Tiger Woods is a good example of this type of regret. Earl Woods, Tiger's father attempted to break into the segregated world of professional golf and failed. Instead of growing bitter, he used his experience as a challenge to mold Tiger into such a remarkable player that his presence would be petitioned rather than shunned. This is a more agreeable form of regret that can bring harmony, rather than discord, into your life.

We regret certain life experiences. Some people regret their financial place in the world. Regretting that you were not born with a silver spoon in your mouth is akin to spitting in the ocean and expecting a change in water volume. Your birth circumstances can't be changed. What *can* change is what you do with your life choices. Many people have lived their dreams, regardless of their birth circumstances, including Sir Winston Churchill, Benjamin Franklin, Maya Angelou, Hilary Swank, Oprah Winfrey, and Jamie Foxx.

Once you have taken the first steps in pursuing your dream, the avenues for paying for your dream will become clear. There is no lack of money in the universe; it is not totally possessed by the rich. You have to investigate money sources, and you have to be open to opportunities that may seek you. Talk to people about your dream. The more people you talk to, the more the universe realizes your dedication to your dream. The money you need will find its way to you if you talk to enough of the right people!

You may realize that you don't need as much money as you first thought when you began your planning. I often have found less expensive ways to get my books published and my business cards and brochures printed through talking to others about my dreams. When you pursue your dream in earnest, doors open that will help you succeed. This may sound like a foreign concept at this point; however, once you have set your foot on the path, you will have interesting stories to share about amazing coincidences.

You have met the Pretenders and examined their voices. They can be powerful, but not empowering, and they must be silenced. It is imperative that you recognize the Pretenders that have limited your access to your dream. Decide today that they will no longer play a role in your life. In the following chapters, we will examine the empowering tools that will enable you to ignore the Pretenders and, eventually, to drive them away.

The exercise that follows will help you determine who your Pretenders are.

Exercise—Finding Your Pretenders

Use these two sheets of paper to write for exactly three minutes. This exercise, once it is started, should be accomplished without raising your pen or pencil from the paper.

If I pursue my dream, I am afraid of

Part II
Learning

Putting Your Choices into Action

"If you keep saying things are going to be bad, you have a good chance of being a prophet."

Isaac Bashevis Singer
Writer and winner of Nobel Prize in Literature
1978

Taking Your Power

Seizing the Moment by Moment by Moment!

"The truth is that we can learn to condition our minds, bodies, and emotions to link pain or pleasure to whatever we choose. By changing what we link pain and pleasure to, we will instantly change our behaviors."

Anthony Robbins

You have now exposed the Pretenders that have challenged your efforts to follow your dream. The exercise at the end of the last chapter helped you identify your own personal fears.

You may find yourself adding new thoughts to those pages as you proceed further into this book.

What can you do to win the challenge of the Pretenders and remain on the path that leads to your dreams? Realize that you have the key! You have taken the first step toward identifying the limiting thoughts that keep you from trusting life on the Green Path. Shining a light on the Pretenders and their intentions is merely the first step toward attaining your goals. There is more to do before you can claim success.

I will start with a quick review of the three paths:

Checkered Path—You choose not to choose. The Pretenders have free reign and appear at will to keep you on a path that offers no consistency and little joy. Good things happen in your life but the good times are fleeting and unplanned. You never know what to expect from one day to the next. Unconscious choice rules.

Yellow Path—You choose yesterday over and over again. You have chosen one or two Pretenders and they have taken up permanent residence in your mind. You are living a 'good' life with bright spots when you plan activities like vacations or go to concerts. You long for more but you would have to welcome change into your life. Unconscious living by conscious choice.

Green Path—You make choices that contribute to living your best life and your dream. The Pretenders continue to try to influence your decisions but you recognize their tactics and keep them at bay. Your goal is to live your best life which is your dream life—being actively engaged in fulfilling your purpose. Conscious choices are weighed for the effect on living your dream life.

More work is required before you can take up residency on the Green Path. Merely identifying the Pretenders won't cause them to disappear. At this point, they are merely quiet. They are reenergizing, getting ready to bring out bigger guns. You are prepared for their attacks. Recognizing your personal birthright to succeed is the next step in quieting the Pretenders.

Deep down you know and believe that you were created to live with purpose. You have a personal birthright to succeed. Unfortunately, calling on the strength of this birthright may have been stymied in childhood by your family, in high school by your peers, or as an adult by your spouse. Regardless of any intentions to squelch it, your birthright to succeed is still there, ready to be accessed as one of your greatest strengths.

Three things have an enormous impact on the direction your life will take: the thoughts you repeatedly think, the power of the words you speak, and the actions that you take through the power of choice.

Recognize that life is not merely a dream state in which we drift step by step from birth to death. Discover the purpose for your life and refuse to allow the Pretenders or others in your life to squelch your dream. Be fully aware of the choices you make and the path you choose daily. Choose the Green Path and choose to live your best life.

In the next chapter, we will address the changes you need to make to begin leading your dream life.

The Power of Words
What Did You Say?

"There was a man who wandered throughout the world seeking the fulfillment of his deepest desires and the greatest of happiness. But, in all of his wanderings, he did not come to it. At last, tired from his arduous journey, he sat beneath a great tree at the foot of a mountain, which, unbeknownst to him, was the Great Wish-Fulfilling Tree.

As he rested beneath the tree, he said, "It is so beautiful here. I wish I had a home on this very spot." And, instantly, a lovely home appeared. The man was delightfully surprised, and he said, "Ah, if only I had a wife to join me, then my happiness would be complete." And, with that, a beautiful woman approached, calling him "my dear husband" and other endearments. "First things first," he said. "I am hungry, and I wish there was food to eat." Immediately, a banquet table, covered with the most exquisite dishes and delicacies, appeared before him. He hungrily began to feast, but, still tired, he said, "I wish I had a servant to wait on me." The servant, too, promptly appeared.

His meal complete, the man leaned against the great tree, and said, "How marvelous! Everything I wish for comes true. There must be a mysterious power in this tree. I wonder if some kind of demon lives in it." And, with that thought, a great demon came forth. "Oh," the man screamed, "this demon will probably devour me!" And, that is precisely what the demon did.

A Traditional Hindu Story

You may never discover a Wish-Fulfilling Tree; however, conscious control over your thoughts and words are essential to your success in living your dreams. No one dreams about living in a negative environment, surrounded by negative people. And no one dreams about not succeeding. Yet, this is how many people live their lives.

Whether you like it or not, your use of words and thoughts, combined with your choices, produce the world that surrounds you. Thoughts are just ideas and dreams until you put them into words to express your intentions.

Words are so powerful in the scheme of the world that the use of words separates man from animals. They are powerful tools that create reality, much like the words of the man in the earlier fable. Luckily, the reality that springs from your thoughts into words is not manifested instantly as in the story. Instead, it comes to fruition over time. As with many things, there is a duality. Positive words of reinforcement build you up; negative words slowly destroy your sense of well-being and your self-esteem. It does not matter whether the words are spoken from your own lips or someone else's, the effect is the same.

Unless you have lived an extremely charmed life, you're intimately associated with the negative power of words. Gossip, slander, and lies are some of the forms negative words can take. Many lives and reputations have been destroyed by the words of others. Words are so powerful that, if several people over time were to mention that you appear ill, you would begin to feel ill, especially if you trust the speakers!

"When you believe something, you have made it true for you."

Excerpt from *A Course in Miracles*

The misuse of words can also have a long-term impact. It is quite possible the misuse of words has already impacted your beliefs and behaviors. Perhaps the limiting words of others have curtailed your dreams. Words callously spoken by parents, teachers, or childhood friends can leave searing scars on the soul. Words can convince you that you are unattractive, untalented, and unworthy.

Words embed themselves in your mind and travel with you. As a result, your actions often validate the words you have chosen to believe.

Search your childhood for words that proved to be unforgettable and prophetic in your life. You have the power to reverse the spell they cast by using your own words to denounce their authenticity.

How can you do this? By thinking and speaking positively about yourself and your ambitions. What you focus on increases in your life. As you have seen, your thoughts and words have a creative power that gives form to the formless energy that surrounds you. When you think or speak negatively about yourself, your body, your talents, or your intellect, you create the channel for circumstances that will confirm those words.

Your thoughts, bundled with your words, become your reality.

Every dream, whether it is a dance, a book, an invention, a speech, or a painting, begins with a thought that is followed by words. When you choose to control your thoughts and words and focus on a specific goal, you're in full control. You may encounter obstacles, but they won't alter your path. You will no longer be a victim of circumstance when you can visualize your future. Think carefully about the person you want to become because you ultimately become the person in your thoughts!

Exercise—Breaking the Negative Cycle

When a negative or self-deprecating thought enters your head, scream, "Stop!" Immediately replace that negative thought with a positive, self-affirming thought or phrase. It can be an affirmation of faith or power. Scream, "Stop", when you are alone and no one can hear you. Mentally scream, "Stop", when you are not alone. These actions, both mentally and physically, have been proven to be extremely successful in redirecting negative thoughts to positive ones before they become negative actions. Remember, it takes twenty-one days to break a habit. Do this whenever a negative thought enters your mind. Eventually, it will become a habit.

Always think and say what you want, not what you don't want!

You can begin right now to consciously change your thought patterns to support positive life experiences, so that you can begin to live your dreams. You are not a powerless spectator in your life. You are a powerful initiator. <u>Proudly announce your dreams to the supporters in your life.</u> Let the world know that you and your dream have arrived on the scene. Positive words and thoughts will put the Pretenders on notice to remain silent, because your positive thoughts have pushed them aside.

Exercise—Unearthing Your Dream

Who did you envision yourself to be after high school or college?

Who are you now?

At what point did you alter your path?

Which Pretender voices played in your head?

What would you like to be doing in two years?

[handwritten notes:] exclusive Lake Travis / finish out / views forever - water - water access / more than 1 BR down / kitchen w/ seating area / large bar / wine room/area / media area / windows everywhere / views / outdoor living / kitchen / views / swim up bar in Pool / Hot tub / office w/ views / amazing / master bath / views / master closet / up - / 2 BR D&B / living - / bar kitchen

Your Personal Birthright

Born to Lose—Not!

"I've learned that the resources we need to turn our dreams into reality are within us, merely waiting for the day when we decide to wake up and claim our birthright."

Anthony Robbins

You have a personal birthright to succeed. Whatever you call your higher power—God, Allah, Yahweh, or Jehovah—know that you have been given the power to succeed. Life never challenges you beyond your capabilities, but it always challenges you to your capacity. Here is an excerpt from Marianne Williamson, author of the bestseller *A Return to Love,*

Our deepest fear is not that we are inadequate. Our deepest fear is that we are powerful beyond measure. It is our light, not our darkness, that most frightens us.

We ask ourselves, who am I to be brilliant, gorgeous, talented and fabulous? Actually, who are you not to be? You are a child of God. Your playing small doesn't serve the world. There is nothing enlightened about shrinking, so that other people won't feel insecure around you.

We are born to make manifest the Glory of God that is within us. It's not just in some of us, it's in everyone, and as we let our own light shine, we consciously give other people permission to do the same. As we are liberated from our own fear, our presence automatically liberates others.

You carry around a picture of yourself commonly called your self-image. This self-image forges the decisions you make, the limitations you place on your life, and your attitude toward change. You can choose to magnify your weaknesses or your strengths. No one is perfect. Accept your perceived imperfections and change your self-image. Don't focus on who you are now—focus on who you will become. The only person who can limit your possibilities is you. You begin to change when you focus on your abilities and how they can contribute to living your dream.

> You can choose to magnify your weaknesses or your strengths.

You have a divine right to succeed and flourish. Why are you rejecting this most precious right? Who wins because you choose not to choose? What is the legacy that you will leave for your children, family, community, and the world? Become a point of light in this world for your immediate community. Are you afraid? Are you too shy?

Fear and shyness flee the scene when confronted by confidence in your own personal power. It does not matter if your dream is big or small; it deserves to see the light of day. You deserve to live your dream, but first there is a little housekeeping that needs to take place.

Purging Your Environment

Lose the Losers

"Nothing can hurt you, unless you give it the power to do so."

Gifts from A Course in Miracles

To succeed, you must first rid your environment of the people and habits that limit your ambitions. Analyze your current relationships: romantic, personal, and professional. Ask yourself the following three questions about each relationship:

- ❑   "Does this person support my dreams?"
- ❑   "Do I experience fear at the thought of mentioning my dream to this person?"
- ❑   "Does this person like me for the individual I am?"

If your answer is no to any of these questions, you should reevaluate the need for these people in your life. You can't eliminate parents, children, and spouses, but you can filter the information you share with them, so they don't contaminate your dream with limiting thoughts or words.

This is a wake-up call to take a closer look at your relationships. Friends and casual relationships that are not supportive of you moving ahead should be replaced with more supportive relationships. It is much easier to move ahead in life if you don't constantly have to prove your ideas or your worth to the people in your life. People who aren't supportive are usually toxic. Toxic people introduce their private fears into your life for many reasons. They pretend to have your best interests at heart (like the Pretenders), but be aware that quite often it is their own interests that really matter to them.

Imagine for a moment that your life is a movie and that you control the characters and the script. Everyone else is also writing their own movie. Ask yourself if you are including the negative people in your movie, or if they are simply overlapping their movie into yours. If they are writing themselves into your movie, they are using your weaknesses to fuel a feeling of power in their own lives. Once you have succeeded in living your dreams and they can no longer use you, these people will fade away into the sunset. Why not write them out of your movie today?

Another toxin that limits your life is unforgiveness. Refusing to forgive and move forward adds weight to your life. Forgiveness is a choice. If you don't forgive, that unforgiveness becomes an act of sabotage. Instead of focusing on your power and talent, you tether yourself to a cycle of misery and pain. It is difficult to move ahead with hurt, grief, or pain weighing you down. Nonetheless, no matter how great the loss or how grievous the offense you experienced, it happened and there is nothing you can do to change it.

There is no truer statement than "The past is dead." You needn't be manipulated by it or continue to rekindle experiences that keep the pain alive. All experiences are learning experiences. Extract the lesson, grieve your loss, and plan your future.

My friend Janice's husband of twenty-five years left her for another woman. The breakup had been sudden and hurtful. Janice was a talented cook. She had always wanted to open a catering business, but her husband had refused to support the venture. After the divorce, Janice refused to forgive or forget, and she refused to move forward with her life.

Her children encouraged her to enroll in a cooking school to pursue her passion. She refused and continued to choose to live in a state of unforgiving bitterness. It was not a state of hope because her former husband had a new family and did not plan to return to her. As a result of the divorce, Janice had the financial means to attend school and live her dream. Instead, she chose to remind herself daily of the hurt she had suffered.

Janice chose a cycle in which she was hurting herself—not her ex-husband—by refusing to move forward in her life. Tragically, Janice died five years after the divorce, still holding onto a dream that she would not pursue because her chosen burdens of pain and anger were too heavy for her to move forward.

Often, people who are miserable have invested their time in holding onto their pain. If you choose to do so, you will keep repeating the same mistakes and continuously find yourself in painful situations until you listen to your inner feelings of success.

Life often hurts. You can choose to relive the hurt over and over or you can choose to file it under experience and, after mourning your loss, move ahead with your plans. Many dreams are given birth after great tragedies. The important concept to note is that moving ahead without constantly reliving the past is a choice.

The familiar saying, "To err is human, to forgive is divine," takes on new meaning. Admit your inability to totally, truly forgive, and hand your plight over to a higher power—then forget and be relieved of the hurt.

Choose to move forward and drop the heavy burden of unforgiveness. It is a toxin that can limit your dreams because you're looking backward when you should be looking forward toward a future that you can influence. Purge your environment of toxic people and emotions. This will leave room for you to develop the positive emotion—passion.

Passion

Turning the Midnight Oil into an Eternal Flame!

"It's the constant and determined effort that breaks down resistance, sweeps away all obstacles."

Claude M. Bristol

Passion is a positive emotion that ushers in a spirit of change. Your passion to succeed in living your dream will give you the impetus to overcome any obstacles that life presents. After you have consciously changed your thoughts and words and have removed the toxic people and behaviors from your life, the way will be clear for passion to blossom, so that you can start living your dream.

55

Passion will drive you forward and refuse to allow you to be indifferent to your inner yearnings. You can develop new, supporting habits to replace the old, restricting ones. A healthy passion won't allow you to ignore family, community, and friends. It will steer you away from activities that don't contribute to your general well-being or the pursuit of your passion.

As you actively pursue your dream, you will notice positive changes in your life. Your interests will be focused on your dream, and it will seem like the entire universe has purchased a ticket for the ride. Supportive people will enter your life. You will get new ideas that will enhance your dream. The best change will be in you. You will look forward to each day and have no problem keeping the past in perspective. Even the toxic people who still remain in your life will drift away to avoid your uplifting conversations and the fact that you no longer have an attitude of meekness.

In the general scheme of the world, the challenge of money may rear its ugly head. Don't allow fear to halt your progress. The money for your dream is available. However, you may have to be persistent about obtaining it!

When I decided to seriously pursue writing after pretending to be interested for more than thirty years, I needed a forward thrust. I decided to enroll in a writing course. My first formidable wall was the cost. I hesitated to inquire about the cost because I imagined it would be four times the actual cost. Once I inquired, I discovered that it was a lot less than I expected, and they also offered a monthly payment plan. I seized the opportunity to pursue my dream.

Dreamers are not new to this universe, nor are their concerns about money to finance their dreams. Your commitment to your vision will draw the resources, opportunities, and energy you need to make your dream a reality.

> *"Enthusiasm is one of the most powerful engines of success. When you do a thing, do it with all your might. Put your whole soul into it. Stamp it with your own personality. Be active, be energetic and faithful, and you will accomplish your object. Nothing great was ever achieved without enthusiasm."*
>
> Ralph Waldo Emerson

Your life is your masterwork—it's the world you're creating and it's also your mirror. Look into it, and you will see clearly and accurately what you're choosing and what you need to change. Heal your inner life and everything else will come into balance. If you are unhappy, get to the source of your pain and create something better.

You're on a train headed directly for your dreams and success.

Personal Power

You're the One!

"You, who perceive yourself as weak and frail, with futile hopes and devastated dreams, born but to die, to weep, and suffer pain, hear this: All power is given unto you in earth and Heaven, there is nothing that you cannot do."

Gifts from A Course in Miracles

You have personal, unlimited power given to you by your Creator. You must stop putting limits on yourself. Remember, life never challenges you beyond your abilities, but always to your capacity. You have to trust your inner resources to become more than you were before. Since all human beings use only a fraction of their abilities, you will never be limited in your growth. Your life works when you find what you have and use it. When you do your part, serenity, security, and success become yours. Failing to live up to who you are causes suffering, which, in essence, is the wake-up call to becoming who you were meant to be. Use your mind to create your own possibilities. Ask yourself: Are my thoughts bountiful enough? Are my words positive enough? Will I take the time to develop a timeline and strategy? It's your business alone to make your life a success. Practice nourishing your dreams everyday, and keep them alive in the nonmaterial world while using your creative intelligence—the great power within—to bring them to fruition.

Dedicate yourself each day to holding a vision in your mind of what you want. Believe in it and nourish it. Know that infinite riches are within and all around you. Take from the treasure trove what you need each day to live confidently, comfortably, and peacefully. Rededicate yourself to your physical, spiritual, and emotional wellness. Give the best of you to yourself. Then you will give the best you have to others. Nothing can stop you when you're focused and refuse to put limits on yourself. For better or worse, you create your future by the choices you make each day.

Bad habits are your worst enemies. Nothing is more detrimental than saying you want to live one way, while you act in ways that produce the opposite results. The blessing is that no matter how ingrained or debilitating a habit is, it can be broken.

To really know what you should be doing, become aware of what's going on within and around you. Ask yourself these questions:

- ❏ Am I doing what I love?
- ❏ Am I happy with where and how I spend my days?
- ❏ Do I like the people I interact with?
- ❏ What would I do if money, security, and power weren't issues?

To settle for unhappiness in *any* area of your life is to miss the whole purpose of living! The personal dramas that make you anxious are the Creator's way of encouraging you to reach, stretch, and grow. Life gives you certain experiences to develop the wisdom, courage, and strength you need to fulfill your purpose. It is up to you to use your unique talents not only for your personal good, but also for the collective good.

The steps necessary to propel your life forward can be summed up as follows:

- ❏ Decide what you want to accomplish.
- ❏ Conduct an honest self-assessment.
- ❏ Let others know what you need.
- ❏ Get rid of the toxins in your life.
- ❏ Embrace the spirit of change.
- ❏ Work in a profession you love.
- ❏ Set a reasonable timeline for you to achieve your dream.

Exercise—Visualizing Your Dream

Find someplace where you can be alone. Take a deep breath and carefully describe the living version of your dream. Make it as detailed as possible. Where will you be living? Who will your life companions be? What will you do daily? Describe the feeling of peace, happiness, or joy that will accompany living your dream. Write until the vision fades. Reread it aloud.

The Power of Love

The Beginning of Authentic Power

"The most authentic thing about us is our capacity to create, to overcome, to endure, to transform. To love and to be greater than our suffering,"

Ben Okri

One evening I watched the movie *March of the Penguins*. I remain in awe of the attention and love between the penguins, if only for a season. The movie explains that male and female penguins mate each season and remain monogamous for that season. The movie also highlights a beautiful scene in which the male and female coo and caress each other with their respective bills; their touch reminded me of a gentle caress. They mate in the harshest of climates after completing a seventy-mile walk to their nesting site. Once they have completed the mating cycle and an egg is produced, the real magic of love begins.

The female penguin shelters the egg between her legs, underneath a pouch of fur for protection. Although the adult penguins can stand the extreme cold, the eggs must be kept warm at all times. The female, after a time, must make the seventy-mile trek back to the sea for food for her and for the chick that will be born during her absence. The egg is precariously passed from mother to father for safekeeping. The exchange is quite difficult and can result in dropping the egg—sudden death for the chick.

While the mother is away, the male penguins huddle together to survive the harsh elements while protecting the eggs. The males have existed for up to four months without food of any kind. When the females return two months later, the chicks are passed from father to mother and the difficult dance begins again. The males, who have lost more than half their body weight, begin the long trek back to the sea for food.

The movie points out that the adults will return to the sea five different times to feed themselves and their offspring. The entire process is a task of love and survival that leaves the audience almost speechless.

The power of love is life-transforming and will eliminate many of the limiting factors in your life. Wherever there is a lack of love, limitations and fear exist. You must learn to love and accept yourself and to love life and those who travel through your life.

When you abandon love, you abandon hope. A hopeless life is lived on the Checkered Path because you trust nothing, including your own instincts. Life is lived day-by-day, but not in honor of the present moment. It is impossible to live in the moment because of a lack of trust. You must constantly project a negative tomorrow and reflect on a dissatisfying yesterday.

You have the choice to choose love over hatred at every moment. Choose to love, and your blessings will begin to surface immediately. Never allow the lack of love reflected from others to change your stance of love. Follow the Golden Rule and your love can work miracles on others and attract supporters and mentors.

During my research for this book, I found a translation of the Golden Rule for twenty-one of the world's religions, compiled by Larry Snyder, who is also known as the Peace Eagle. It is interesting to see how many other religions have a Golden Rule, similar to the one found in Matthew 7:12, "Do to others what you would have them do to you" (NIV). Here are a few examples:

Bahá'i World Faith
"Ascribe not to any soul that which thou wouldst not have ascribed to thee, and say not that which thou doest not. Blessed is he who preferreth his brother before himself."

—*Bahá'u'lláh*

Buddhism

"A state that is not pleasing or delightful to me, how could I inflict that upon another?"

—*Samyutta Nikaya v. 353*

Hinduism

"One should not behave towards others in a way which is disagreeable to oneself."

—*Mencius VII.A.4*

"This is the sum of the Dharma [duty]: do naught unto others which would cause you pain if done to you."

—*Mahabharata 5:1517*

Islam

"None of you [truly] believes until he wishes for his brother what he wishes for himself."

—Number 13 of Imam "Al-Nawawi's Forty Hadiths"

Judaism

"Thou shalt love thy neighbor as thyself."

—*Leviticus 19:18 (KJV)*

"What is hateful to you, do not to your fellow man. This is the law: all the rest is commentary."

—*Talmud, Shabbat 31a*

Unitarian

"We affirm and promote respect for the interdependent of all existence of which we are a part."

—Unitarian principles.

Love is a single thread that has tracked through history and triumphed time and again. War and hatred have also tracked through history. Neither war nor hatred has left a legacy of hope or eternity. Hatred meeting hatred is akin to two warlords replacing each other as overseers of a country.

Design your dream with love, to honor, love, and help others. The universe will rush angels to your side to push your dream forward.

Part III
Being

Living Your Dream Life

"Build this day on a foundation of pleasant thoughts. Never fret at any imperfections that you fear may impede your progress. Remind yourself, as often as necessary, that you are a creature of God and have the power to achieve any dream by lifting up your thoughts. You can fly, when you decide that you can. Never consider yourself defeated again. Let the vision in your heart be in your life's blueprint. Smile!"

Og Mandino
Inspirational speaker and author

Choosing the Right Path
Stepping into a New Life

"The doors we open and close each day decide the lives we live."

Flora Whittemore

You have learned to challenge and in some cases banish the Pretenders, taken back your personal power, began to remove negative people and their influences from your life, and set a plan in motion to achieve your dream. More importantly, you now have a clearer vision of your dream and the joy it will add to your life. Hold on tight and get ready for a wild ride! Your newly found passion will need to survive several roller coaster rides.

Each day begins with an eye toward inching closer to living your dream life. If you have lived as I had on the Yellow

Path for years, each new day now begins with an air of excitement that you embrace. This air of excitement is the 'newness' of living life with purpose. Having and meeting your goals for a day will also allow you to sleep better than you have in years because there is peace in accomplishment. The excitement comes from recognizing the choices you make and basking in a newfound appreciation of 'you'.

On the flip side, welcoming change into a life that is either staid from living on the Yellow Path or unfocused from living on the Checkered Path will require some adjustments. Stay focused by having a written plan of action and a vision of your next step.

It is at this point that some choose to retreat back to their familiar paths. The Pretenders win and the old familiar paths appear to be safer. They are not safer, only familiar. By retreating you are often choosing to live a 'good' life versus your 'best' life. You deserve the best as your Creator intended. You are reading this book because your spirit longs for more out of life.

Embrace the spirit of change as doors open to support your new life's vision. The first area of your new life that will need close attention is your attitude. Everyday is a new day and an opportunity to choose a new attitude. The attitude you choose can either inspire your actions or erect both real and imaginary boundaries. When you choose to take the Green Path, you are accepting an attitude that welcomes change and all of its ramifications.

Seeing Beyond What Is

Visions of Deserved Grandeur

"Dream lofty dreams, and as you dream, so shall you become. Your Vision is the promise of what you shall one day be. Your Ideal is the prophecy of what you shall at last unveil."

James Allen

The first step you need to take to live your dream life is in perfecting your vision of your life as you live your dream. Too often, we ignore our natural talents because we refuse to accept a life other than the one we now lead. Dream *big!* Dream *now!* See yourself actually living your dream. It is very easy to start a dream and then allow your old self-

73

defeating habits to take the reins. I should know because it happened to me.

In 1999, I developed a passion for Alexander Pushkin, a Russian genius who lived during the Czarist period of Russian history. I compiled volumes of research and read every English translation of Pushkin's work that was available. I had a burning desire to share my discovery of this brilliant and misunderstood man with the world. After more than three years of study and hundreds of pages of written material, I abandoned the project. Why? Because all of the books that had been written to date were written by well-known historians whom I felt would mock my efforts. The voices of the Pretenders were loud and clear:

- ❑ "Who do you think you are?"
- ❑ "You will be laughed out of the industry."
- ❑ "What are your writing credentials?"
- ❑ "No one will take you seriously."

The list filled two pages. I shelved the project, although my reader, a history professor, loved my story, and two audiences to whom I presented it were mesmerized and begged me to return when the book was finished. I failed to see myself actually living the dream of releasing the story. To complete my self-sabotage, I sent a proposal to several agents and editors who completed the job of the Pretenders.

I visualized myself writing the book, but I failed to visualize myself successfully selling it. What I also failed to realize was that I was not writing the book for academia or as an expert. I was introducing an intriguing, full-dimension character to the world. This is more evidence that the Pretenders can throw you so off balance that you fail to make sense of your motives. In the end, I chose my doubts over my dreams and continued to live on the Yellow Path.

Because I wanted to help others, I immediately saw myself successfully writing and selling this book, *Three Paths, Three Choices*. This self-visualization kept me from abandoning the project. You too can live your dream by visualizing it in detail and seeing beyond what you can see today. Have faith in your potential.

Attitude

Taking Charge and Taking Names

"People are always blaming their circumstances for what they are. I don't believe in circumstances. The people who get on in this world are the people who get up and look for the circumstances they want, and, if they can't find them, make them."

George Bernard Shaw,
Mrs. Warren's Profession, 1893

You've prepared your heart, mind, and intention. It is time to take the first step toward living your dream. Taking risks is a requirement and, as we all know, risk taking can be frightening. However, you're now prepared. There is an old saying, "When preparation meets fear, it becomes courage." At this point, you are recognizing any limiting voices and at the same time recognizing the true intent of these voices. You must have a positive and accepting attitude as you travel the road to success.

Why is your attitude so important? Like it or not, your attitude determines your ability to maintain your action plan. It's hard work to establish an action plan, and it is only the first step. You must fortify your plan to withstand challenges to its right to exist. Old antagonists will not simply disappear; they will often grow stronger and appear more often in your life. Therefore, the most significant and important decision you make each day is choosing your attitude.

Your attitude is even more important than your finances, your past experiences, your education, or your dreams. When you choose to confront daily challenges with confidence, your plan will begin to unfold and you will find opportunities. You can choose to accept any challenges as opportunities that will teach you more about your goal and about yourself.

Attitude and perception are tightly woven. During my first visit to Jamaica, I had a lesson in differing attitudes in the perception of weather. I, along with about fifty other tourists, was sitting on one of the local beaches enjoying the surf, sun and music. Local teenagers were playing volleyball about twenty feet way. It was a perfect day in paradise when it began to rain. The rain was heavy and sudden. All of the tourists began shrieking and running for the nearest shelter. We were all wet and hiding under a huge tent. I looked out toward the beach and the teenagers were still playing volleyball. They had never stopped playing. I was forced to look at my attitude toward rain. Why did I run? I was already soaking wet but neither I nor any of the other tourists budged until the rain stopped. The locals saw the rain as welcoming and natural. My learned attitude toward rain was not only to run for cover, but also to dread its appearance although the earth needs rain to survive. Attitude is often a learned response. Since that day on the beach, I have learned to welcome rain as a friend rather than a foe.

How many of your attitudes are learned responses? Learned responses can be reprogrammed. Your choice of attitude can keep you going or can cripple your progress. It is truly up to you!

Now that you've chosen the Green Path and have developed a confident attitude, you need to develop an action plan that will help you reach your goals. The length and complexity of your plan is determined by the complexity of your dream. Let's use the example of piano playing to illustrate a possible action plan. Remember that each dream requires different actions.

Dream #1—to play the piano well enough to entertain your friends and family. Where will you play? In your home? In a club? In church? Previous training: none. Tools needed: a piano. Working Plan: to contact a reputable instructor to begin lessons.

Note: After your initial investigation, if you decide to proceed after contacting an instructor, purchase or rent a piano, set aside time to practice etc.

Dream #2—to learn to play the piano well enough to give concert performances on stage. You will start with the same basic needs as Plan A; however, your plan will involve more extensive training. Previous training: none. Skills needed: extensive training in music theory. Enroll in a suitable educational facility. Purchase a piano. Prepare for years of intensive training, practice, and competition. Restructure your life to accommodate your aspirations.

These two dreams are similar only in the most basic concept: to learn to play the piano. The action plans are different because each is based on the ultimate goal for acquiring the skill. Both dreams are attainable, regardless of your age. However, the structure needed to attain each dream differs according to its complexity.

Use the dream mapping exercise that follows to map out your dream. As you delve deeper into living your dream, realize that the parameters will change as you discover new information that will help you support your dream.

For now, make a living action plan for your dream.

Exercise: Mapping My Dream

(This is your plan as you see it today)

My dream

Previous experience

Tools Needed

Additional education needed

Contacts I already have (if needed)

Contacts I need to develop

Time required in my daily life

Family support needed

Financial support needed

Time line of first phase

Read your plan aloud. Add new ideas as needed. Read it daily to keep your plan in focus.

To illustrate the flexibility of your plan, use the following suggestions to add new dimensions to it:

Network with those who have the job you want. This allows you to double-check your impressions about your dream. It will also give you an opportunity to refine your assessment of the tools and education you will need to achieve your dream. You may meet a mentor from this step. **Warning**: This step should never cancel your dream. This fact gathering should only give you a clearer picture of the different aspects of your dream life. You may choose to fulfill your dream in an entirely different way from the person you are interviewing, or you may, during the course of the interview, stumble upon a new direction for your dream. Never give up. This is *your* dream.

Clear the clutter. It is difficult to think clearly when you are surrounded by clutter. Clear your personal work area of any unneeded papers and files. Keep a designated pad of paper to jot down new ideas. Maintain a calendar to chart your progress, make appointments, and organize your life. How willing would an investor be if your work area is overrun with papers and files? What if it took you more than ten minutes to find the correct file to discuss the idea? I think you get the picture.

Get more education. To accomplish your dream, you may need more formal education or training. Get the facts. Learn what the financial obligations may be, and find out about available financial assistance programs.

Pay your dues—you will not start at the top. There are no overnight success stories. Fulfilling your dream will require hard work and perseverance. Begin slowly and develop an expertise in your chosen field.

Trust in faith and prayer. You will need both on days when obstacles seem to be overwhelming. You are the only one who can cancel your dream. Believe in your right to live your dream and persevere. Remember, in hindsight, obstacles never seem as large as when they first appeared.

Volunteer or be an apprentice to get a sense of what the job entails. This is an excellent way to begin in many fields. By working as a volunteer or apprentice, you develop mentors and get a sense of what the work is like, along with an opportunity to contribute.

Know what employers want. If a job or career in a specific industry is your goal, you must be prepared. Read that industry's literature. Schedule appointments with human resource personnel to find out what it takes to get the job you want. It's a good thing that you overcame your shyness in Chapter 1. Be aggressive about pursuing your dream.

Take a risk. Nothing in life is gained without risk. Not taking a risk has probably kept your dream on hold for years. Take a risk and breathe life into your dream.

Cultivate mentors. A relationship with a mentor is invaluable. It cuts corners, saves time, and can remove many obstacles. Unless you're charting new territory, someone else is already living your dream. Contact those people by mail, phone, or Internet. Never be discouraged by the few who have no interest in sharing their knowledge. Look at their ingratitude as a blessing, for they would become negative people in your life. Another dream seeker will gladly share time and information with you. Put your energy into finding that person. For a few months, make it your job to locate that person.

Read everything about your new field or dream. Become an expert on your own home turf. Read, attend lectures, and network. The more intimately you know your dream, the more excitement and passion you will have for it. Ignore the voices of the Pretenders. Don't believe them. This is your dream. You can do anything! Also, read the biographies of famous people who were faced with seemingly impossible obstacles. Learn how they came through their darkest hours to triumph and find peace and happiness.

Go with your gut feelings. Last, but not least, be open to supportive information, which may appear in the strangest places. Remember, there are no coincidences. You have given the universe notice by developing your plan, and the universe will send helpful people and information your way. Your job is to be ready to accept these blessings as they appear.

"Self-trust is the first secret of success."

Ralph Waldo Emerson
American author, poet and philosopher

Change

Blessings Dressed in Wolf's Clothing

"Change is the law of life and those who look only to the past or present are certain to miss the future."

John F. Kennedy

The old axiom, "Change is inevitable," becomes more palatable as you create your dream. Try to imagine life without change of any kind—kids would not grow, plants would remain at sprout stage, daily temperatures would be constant, and you would be trapped in repeating days much like Bill

Murray in the movie *Groundhog Day*. Change is not only inevitable, it is constant. Accepting that change is inevitable gives you a new start and a new attitude. As you grow more comfortable with your new attitude, the way you make decisions and the way you prioritize your time will become key elements in forging your new life. Being open to change and all the challenges that accompany it is very important. Remember, you're in charge and the universe is lending its assistance, although often in surprising ways. Remember, *nothing that happens is a coincidence!* Every encounter in your life has significance.

The concept you have envisioned and developed as your dream may only be the tip of the iceberg. Few people set out to change the world, yet there are those who begin their journey to attain a simple goal and it mushrooms into national or international notice. It happens because a dream belongs to both an individual and the universe. Nevertheless, you will still be in charge of your dream, and you can accept or reject any blessings offered. My message is simply to acknowledge that your dream may change in some aspects from your original vision.

You may be familiar with the actress Caryn Johnson who is better known as Whoopi Goldberg. When she was growing up in New York City, Whoopi had a dream of one day appearing on stage. After putting her dream on hold for years, she still dreamed of seeing herself on stage. The problem was the absence of role models who looked even remotely like her. Whoopi took small Broadway parts while working at odd jobs, including as a bricklayer and as a makeup artist in a funeral parlor. Although she dreamed about working on

Broadway, she altered the scene of her dream and joined an improvisational comedy troupe. The group moved to California to perform, and Whoopi took a risk and moved with them, leaving her dream of the Broadway stage behind. The rest is Hollywood history. Whoopi ultimately performed in a one-woman show and landed a part in the movie *The Color Purple.*

The starring movie role and its subsequent recognition led to roles in more than eighty-five movies. She's also made seventy-five guest TV appearances and has co-produced ten movies. Whoopi was nominated for and received an Oscar for her role in the movie *Ghost.*

Eventually, Whoopi returned to Broadway, starring in the play *The Producers.* It was as unlikely a way to achieve her dream as anyone could imagine. After her run on Broadway, Whoopi returned to California and the movies. Perhaps her original dream paled in comparison to the alternate life that evolved.

Whoopi's story illustrates the circuitous route you might take to live out your dream. Because Whoopi was open to change (from Broadway stage to comedy stage), open to taking a risk (moving to California), and open to new ideas (starring in a movie as a newcomer), she eventually achieved her original dream of performing on the Broadway stage.

> *"Unless you are prepared to give up something valuable you will never be able to truly change at all, because you'll be forever in the control of things that you can't give up."*
> Andy Law, *Creative Company*

Follow *your* dream! Be open to change! Welcome the blessings that appear as challenges and detours. The passion you have at the beginning will ebb and flow, but there are ways to sustain a healthy level of passion, as we will see in the next chapter.

Sustaining Passion

Being as Stubborn as Trick Birthday Candles

"Success is not the result of spontaneous combustion. You must set yourself on fire."

Reggie Leach

Passion begins as a burning desire, spreading from your head to your heart and eventually throughout your entire body. Yet, at times, it may simmer to a small flame. This is natural. If you were to sustain the original fires of passion, you would look like a single-minded, out-of-control madman to the rest of the world. Any possible financial supporters or mentors would run at the first appearance of such a zealot. Ultimately, your family would feel deserted, and you would lose touch with what was happening in the world.

Burning passion needs to be balanced to be sustained. Working and focusing all of your energy in a single direction is neither healthy nor productive. If you're alienating those around you, living your dream had better include living alone in a cabin in the woods or living and eating in the basement, surrounded by your great inventions. Many of you won't become overly consumed with passion for your dream. Instead, most of you will, at times, have difficulty sustaining the passion to keep your dream going.

I'm painfully aware of the effects of a loss of passion. When I turned fifty, I decided to pursue my dream of owning a gift store. I was passionate about pursuing business training, securing financing, and setting up the actual business. It was a beautiful store and surpassed my vision of what my gift store would be. Yet shortly after the store opened, my passion waned. I did not join any retail organizations, I did not scout competitive stores, I did not have a mentor, and I tied my personal time to working in the store alone. Needless to say, the gift shop—my dream—closed soon after its first anniversary.

Conversely, Kenny Rogers is a perfect example of sustained passion. He was born in Houston, Texas, in 1938 to non-musical parents. Music became his passion, and he learned to play both guitar and fiddle in high school. He joined his first band in 1956. Having chosen music as his career, he played with a rockabilly band and released three singles. Kenny briefly entered college, then dropped out to pursue his passion. He failed many times over the years before becoming successful.

From the late fifties until the eighties, he joined several singing groups and played backup for other musicians. Several times over the years, success eluded him as he endured band breakups and went into heavy debt. Kenny never gave up. He was open to change.

In 1974, he made a conscious decision to change from contemporary pop to country music. That decision catapulted him to stardom. Kenny went on to win the Country Music Award, star in movies, and start his own restaurant chain. His popularity waned briefly, and he pursued other passions, like photography. He published several books of photos. Music still called his name and, in 1999, Kenny returned to the music world to issue a new wave of hits and to start his own record label, aptly named Dream Catcher!

You can sustain healthy passion for your dream in several ways:

Surround yourself with others who share the same passion or dream. For example, if your dream is to be a writer—join a writer's association or a writer's discussion group, and enroll in writing classes. This will give you an opportunity to exchange ideas with other writers, note the progress of others, and network in the field of your dream.

Subscribe to industry magazines and publications. This will keep you abreast of industry trends and will also keep your imagination alive as you read about and discover gaps in the industry that need to be filled.

Meditate daily about your dream. Remember the power of thoughts and words. Every day you can recite: "I choose to be successful today. I choose to be happy today. I choose to be loved today. I choose to be healthy today. I choose to be prosperous today." Prosperity is not always about money. What is *your* definition of prosperity?

Read motivational books and listen to motivational tapes. These will help you keep the Pretenders at bay by reminding you of your God-given right to be successful, healthy, and happy.

Avoid negative people. If I sound like a broken record, it's because this is too important not to mention again. Negative people strengthen the Pretenders. If your world is inhabited by non-supportive people, tell them good-bye. They have no interest in accompanying you on the road to living your dream because they are not living theirs. If the negative people are your parents, siblings, or spouse, you can *choose* not to discuss your dream with them or in their presence. They will only throw cold water on your passion and dampen your enthusiasm, along with awakening the Pretenders and amplifying their voices. Once your dream comes to fruition, the people who tried their best to discourage you will become your biggest supporters. Everyone loves a winner!

Take long walks and make time for gym workouts and family. This will contribute to your general well-being and prevent passion burnout. If you have more than one dream, spend a portion of your time on another area of development to give you perspective on your progress.

Whatever shows up in your life is a gift. Be open and be ready for changes in the scope of your dream. New ways of looking at your dream can reignite your passion.

Expect the Best and Be Your Best

Eagles, Excellence, and Egos

"There are only two ways to live your life. One is as though nothing is a miracle. The other is as though everything is a miracle."

Albert Einstein

Hilary Swank is an actress whose life personifies the message in this chapter. At the age of thirty, she won two Oscars for Best Actress. Her story begins in a trailer park in Bellingham, Washington. Hilary always dreamed of becoming an actress and, with the assistance of her mother, her dream has come true.

Her Cinderella story began when, at age fifteen, her mother packed up the family car and drove from Washington to Los Angeles with $75 and no place to live. They were homeless for two weeks. Then they were offered a friend's empty house to sleep in at night. During the day, Hilary's mother used a pay phone to call agents for Hilary.

After she hired an agent, Hilary began to get minor roles. Her first big break came when Hilary beat hundreds of other aspiring actresses for a chance to star in the movie *The Next Karate Kid*. By the time she was twenty-three, she had a part in the popular TV series *Beverly Hills 90210*. When she was dropped from the series, Hilary was devastated, but it was a blessing in disguise because she was available to audition for

> *"I don't know what I did in this life to deserve all of this. I'm just a girl from a trailer park who had a dream."*
> Hilary Swank

the leading part in what would be her Oscar-wining role as Tina Brandon in the movie *Boys Don't Cry*. The rest is Hollywood history, and it is still unwinding. Both Hilary and her mother always expected her dreams to come true, and Hilary always backs up her dreams by giving the best performance possible.

You too ultimately live the life you choose and, through your choices, life mirrors not only your expectations, but also the amount of energy you put into meeting those expectations. Decide today to expect only the best opportunities to occur in your life, and also to challenge yourself to make your best effort toward living your dream.

Your best efforts will differ everyday. Don't expect perfection or a certain level of output each day. Your best is dependent on your mood for the day, your level of energy, and the differing levels of support you need from your family on a daily basis. By contributing your best efforts for each day, you will silence the voices of the Pretenders, which masquerade as self-doubt, low self-esteem, and guilt.

When you expect the best from all life situations, you will see a change in your world. Blessings, often labeled as miracles, will become your daily companions. You will begin to notice you only have to speak a desire and it shows up. It won't always appear immediately, but it will show up. This may seem like a strange concept, but if you're open to seeing your desires fulfilled, it will happen.

Confidence—The Dealmaker

Sitting Tall in the Saddle

"Be bold—and mighty forces will come to your aid."

King Basil

If you are familiar with old television Westerns like *Gunsmoke* and movies starring John Wayne, then you are familiar with the sight of a rider sitting tall in the saddle. There are many ways to ride a horse; a slump can signal that a rider is tired or wounded; a lean to the left or right can signal that the horse is out of the rider's control; a rider with his head down is wounded, asleep or weary; and a rider lying across the saddle is dead. The rider sitting tall in the saddle is confident and prepared for action if and when it comes his way.

Having confidence means knowing you have a goal and an action plan. Your sense of confidence will increase daily as you watch your plan unfold and as you understand that you alone are in control through your choices.

Confidence is not arrogance. Arrogance is another face of fear because it is based on creating fear in others and having a limited sense of control of one's own actions. True confidence inspires others and invites imitation.

Donald Trump, the real estate mogul, is the picture of confidence. Although many of

> *"As long as you are going to be thinking anyway, think big."*
> Donald Trump

his business ventures have faced bankruptcy filings, Donald's public display of confidence remains unwavering. Many business owners never rebound from a bankruptcy, either financially or emotionally. While only those close to him may know how he feels about his very public failures, Donald's ability to rise again and again, like the mythological phoenix from the ashes, and his public bravado are inspiring.

> *"The man who has confidence in himself, gains the confidence of others."*
> Hasidic saying

Confidence begets confidence. Reading the biographies of those who have overcome great obstacles and surrounding yourself with confident people are two steps you can take to build your confidence. As your sense of confidence grows, it will be evident in your posture, your face, your speech, and your every move. Supportive people and success may be drawn to your doorstep. When you're confident, you don't just believe you can do it, you *know* you can.

To move from living in a state of fear to living in a state of confidence, you will need practice. Confident people believe in themselves. They take calculated risks, sometimes winning and sometimes losing. You just need to have the courage to take small risks, celebrate each victory, and build the self-trust you need to try for bigger and better opportunities.

Some people develop confidence because they are blessed with loving parents who support their personal growth. Others gain their confidence by starting each day with a ritual of self-love and confidence. This practice not only projects self-love, it also quiets the voices of the Pretenders.

You can develop your own rituals to instill confidence. Here are some examples:

You can begin each day by looking in the mirror at yourself and repeating positive affirmations. (**Note:** Affirmations will differ by person. Your affirmations should address your perceived lack, for example, "I am strong," "I am intelligent," or "I am beautiful.")

I use a daily affirmation written by Donald G. Scott who shared this affirmation with me during a National Speaker's Association meeting and I cherish it.

I AM

I am healthy
I am wealthy
All there is
Is truly mine.

I am intelligent
I am strong
I am pure
I am fine.

I am filled with love
I am full of grace
May GOD Bless
This human face.

Patience is virtue
Truth is right
I Love my GOD
With all my might.

With all my heart
And God's perfection
Progress is seen
In my direction.

Donald Scott
© 1987 by Living Resources

Other suggestions for increasing self-confidence include the following:

❏ Celebrate each small step you take toward your goal.

❏ Toot your own horn to supportive friends.

❏ Love the body you have—it's the only one you will get on this journey.

❏ Love your fellow man: inner peace produces confidence.

❏ Trust that you will be given all you need and that the universe is on your side.

❏ Remember, there are no negative events. Negativity is a challenge and an opportunity to grow in experience.

❏ Examine any perceived setback for its positive repercussions.

❏ Mentor someone who is just starting on their path to living their dream.

❏ Expand your dream and watch the magic of synchronicity.

❏ Readjust your plan as needed.

No Apologies Necessary
A Pinch of Oprah, a Cup of Martha, and Stir

Every decision you make stems from what you think you are, and represents the value that you put upon yourself.

Deep within you is everything that is perfect, ready to radiate through you and out into the world.

Gifts from a Course in Miracles

If you have spent a great deal of your life apologizing for any small success you have achieved, stop it now! Modesty is not a virtue when it involves living your dream. Not only do you deserve your success, you have earned it through careful planning and action.

Modesty and the Pretender shyness will work hand in hand to place stumbling blocks in your path. Being modest has kept me from basking in my momentary glories and from pushing ahead because I had not congratulated myself properly. After my appearance on *The Oprah Winfrey Show,* I told a few people and, when asked about my appearance by others, I smiled shyly and refused to recall it for some very eager listeners. One day, I saw the rapper P. Diddy as a guest on a television show, and his demeanor shocked me. He was so glad to be there that he was gushing and blushing with happiness. As I sat in my living room and pondered his excitement. I wondered why I had been so demure about my experience. Here was a man with millions of dollars and his own successful businesses. He had met many famous people, but this was one of his best moments. I reviewed my reaction and was forced to remember that one of my readers before publishing this book had insisted that I include the Oprah appearance in this book, over my objections.

When I think of a role model for this chapter, Eleanor Roosevelt, wife of former President Franklin D. Roosevelt, instantly comes to mind. While historians have acknowledged her shyness and insecurity, they also have duly noted her determination to speak out on behalf of those

> *"No one can make you feel inferior without your consent."*
> Eleanor Roosevelt

she felt had no voice. She changed the role of the first lady for all time and became the first woman to write a syndicated column, to earn money as a lecturer, to hold regular press conferences, and to speak at a national political convention.

During her time in the public eye, she never faltered or offered apologies for her decisions or choices. Although she lived during a time that demanded that a woman live in the shadow of her husband, she emerged as a symbol of the strength of women. Her refusal to make apologies for her stances enabled her to address issues she identified as unjust. When she realized that women were not being hired as reporters, she organized more than three hundred press conferences restricted to women journalists.

When confronted by the press and her detractors, Eleanor offered lasting, heartfelt words that would become a part of her legacy, instead of making remarks that would have focused on her character and driven the emphasis away from her projects.

Today, there are two powerful women on television who encourage and exemplify the essence of living life without apologies for one's successes in entirely different ways. Oprah Winfrey shows viewers through her actions and the actions of guests, that self-praise is honorable, self-sacrifice is admirable and self-promotion is expected. The other power-house, Martha Stewart, promotes herself as the consummate businesswoman and after being accused, tried, convicted, and freed for the crime of lying during an investigation, she continued to expand and promote her business interests without delay and without apology.

The manner you assume when you accept compliments reflects your level of self-esteem. If you look away, blush, smile sheepishly, or deflect the graciousness of the compliment by stating, "It's really no big deal," or "Anyone could have done it," you need to develop more self-confidence and bravado. You deserve every accolade possible for having a dream, developing an action plan, taking action, and succeeding.

I have accomplished many things in my life, yet I was always so busy looking for the next obstacle, I never took the time, even for a moment, to bask in my own glory. At every step, congratulate yourself. This is what Olympic champions do. It is called "Olympic motivation," and it really works! Chill a bottle of champagne or treat yourself to dinner at your favorite restaurant to celebrate an achievement. Flaunt your success! Frame pictures of successful networking meetings, articles, and letters of gratitude or congratulations. Remind yourself of your achievements, for they have come at a price that only you can tabulate.

If you need to present your idea to a financial advisor, bank, or fellow dreamer, proudly share your vision. This is not the time to hide your passion under a cloak of modesty or shyness. Be bold. Be enthusiastic. This is your dream. Be proud of it!

Gratitude
Alms, Affirmations, and Amens

"No person has ever been honored for what he received. Honor has been the reward for what he gave."

Calvin Coolidge

Being grateful will come naturally as you overcome obstacles and begin to live your dream. As the obstacles fall behind, you will be grateful for each step forward. It is your duty to extend your gratitude to the universe through service to others. You can mentor, volunteer, or give financial support to those organizations whose goals exemplify your deepest-held visions for the world.

Showing your gratitude through service to others is the legacy of your dream. It will live beyond your time, either in the minds of those you have helped through mentoring and volunteerism or in the continuing legacy that financial support renders.

Gratitude becomes your lasting legacy to your loved ones and the world. One of the greatest portraits of this principle can be found in the little known legacy of Benjamin

> *"The use of money is all the advantage there is in having it."*
> Benjamin Franklin

Franklin. We are all familiar with his contributions to the United States Constitution and his many inventions. Yet few know of the lasting monetary gift he left for his new nation. Franklin, who died in 1790, left a codicil in his will of a hundred pounds sterling to the cities of Philadelphia and Boston. It is believed that he chose these two cities because he had been born in Boston and had later adopted Philadelphia as his home.

No stranger to the concept of compound interest, Franklin was well aware of the potential growth of his bequest and left no element of chance in its use. For the first hundred years after his death, it was to be used to make low-interest loans to young tradesmen who were starting a business. After a hundred years, he stipulated that one-quarter would remain to make the loans, but the remaining three-quarters were to be used for public works in each city. After two hundred years, the total was again to be divided, allowing the two cities to keep one-quarter of the total. The rest funneled to the respective states with no restriction on the use of the money.

The bequest, which is now worth millions of dollars, has lasted well into the twenty-first century and is still being used to fund scholarships and to support organizations that address such issues as women's health and disabled children.

Is gratitude important? It forges a public image that can have predictable consequences. The two women mentioned in the previous chapter, Oprah Winfrey and Martha Stewart have both amassed enormous wealth through hard work, ingenuity, and perseverance. They both have television programs and successful magazines. Oprah Winfrey is perceived as being the consummate giver; Martha Stewart is seen as a powerhouse who forges ahead with little regard for others. Their respective media personas reflect the essence of their public generosity. Oprah may not be loved by all, but the public's perception of her as a giver overshadows most negative opinions. Martha may be a generous woman in her own right, but she is not perceived that way by the public. Instead, she is ridiculed and pitied by few.

When I meet my Maker, I like to think that he will ask me two profound questions: "What did you do with what I gave you?" and "What did you leave behind that shows that you were there?" I am building my life choices to answer these questions.

Once you have begun to live your dream, look for ways to help others find or live their dreams. This is true gratitude for the gifts you receive.

There are those who maintain that the poor people of the world will always be poor. I maintain that when givers outnumber takers in society, the poor will become history. Join the ranks of the givers. You have learned firsthand that the universe rewards your efforts, so give back.

"If the only prayer you say in your whole life is 'Thank you,' that would be enough."

Meister Eckhart
German theologian, philosopher and mystic

Parting Words — You Are the Miracle!

That's My Story and I'm Sticking to It!

If you have finished this book and have not begun to plan your dream, then you are waiting for a miracle. The following article, written by Ralph S. Marston in his *Daily Motivator* newsletter, may be of interest to you.

Waiting for a Miracle?

If you are waiting for a miracle, your wait is over. *You* are the miracle. Against all odds, you are here today, alive, filled with possibilities. You can shape the world around you. You can imagine, dream, and create. You can experience, reason, share, and love.

What could possibly be more miraculous than your life? You are at once unique and connected to all of creation. Think for a moment how special you are. Think of the unique expression of life, love, and energy that is you. Think of how far you've already come.

Bibliography

Marston, Ralph S. Jr. *The Daily Motivator* (Confidence).

Gifts from a Course in Miracles. Edited by Frances Vaughan, PhD, and Roger Walsh, MD, PhD, Putnam Books, New York, N.Y., Copyright 1983, 1986, 1988, Introduction Copyright 1995 by Frances Vaughan and Roger Walsh. Foreword by Marianne Williamson.

Zerah, Aaron. Every Day is a Blessing, New York, N.Y., Warner Books, 2002.

For additional copies of

Three Paths, Three Choices

Getting The Life That You Deserve

$12.95 paperback

Visit your favorite bookstore

or fax your order to (512) 292-3693

Quantity discounts available

Visit my Web site: www.sherryransom.com

To book Sherry D. Ransom for speaking engagements contact:

Sherry Ransom Productions
PO Box 326
Manchaca, TX 78652-0326

Telephone: (512) 922-1882
Fax: (512) 292-3693

978-0-595-38537-9
0-595-38537-0

Printed in the United States
60536LVS00001B/82

9 780595 385379